DANICA PATRICK

By Dina El Nabli

People We Should Know

Gareth Stevens
Publishing

Please visit our web site at **www.garethstevens.com**
For a free color catalog describing our list of high-quality books,
call 1-800-542-2595 (USA) or 1-800-387-3178 (Canada). Our fax: 1-877-542-2596

Library of Congress Cataloging-in-Publication Data
El Nabli, Dina.
    Danica Patrick / by Dina El Nabli.
      p. cm. — (People We Should Know)
    Includes bibliographical references and index.
    ISBN-10: 1-4339-0018-1 ISBN-13: 978-1-4339-0018-1 (lib. bdg.)
    ISBN-10: 1-4339-0158-7 ISBN-13: 978-1-4339-0158-4 (soft cover)
    1. Patrick, Danica, 1982—Juvenile literature. 2. Automobile racing drivers—
  United States—Biography—Juvenile literature. 3. Women automobile racing drivers—
  United States—Biography—Juvenile literature. I. Title.
  GV1032.P38E4 2009
  796.72092—dc22 [B]   2008039871

This edition first published in 2009 by
Gareth Stevens Publishing
A Weekly Reader® Company
1 Reader's Digest Road
Pleasantville, NY 10570-7000 USA

Executive Managing Editor: Lisa M. Herrington
Senior Editor: Brian Fitzgerald
Associate Editor: Amanda Hudson
Creative Director: Lisa Donovan
Senior Designer: Keith Plechaty
Photo Researcher: Kim Babbitt
Publisher: Keith Garton

Picture credits
Cover and title page: Gavin Lawrence/Getty Images; p. 5: AFP/Getty Images; p. 7: Jonathan
Ferrey/Getty Images; pp. 9, 10, 13, 14: Courtesy of the Patrick Family; p. 15: George
Tiedemann/Corbis; p. 17: Michael Kim/Corbis; pp. 18, 22: Paul Webb Photography; p. 19:
Robert Laberge/Getty Images; p. 20: AP Images; p. 21: Donald Miralle/Getty Images; p. 25:
KMazur/Getty Images; p. 26: Andrew Malana/Corbis; p. 28: Jeff Haynes/AFP/Getty Images.

Printed in the United States of America

1 2 3 4 5 6 7 8 9 10 09 08

TABLE OF CONTENTS

Words in the glossary appear in **bold** type
the first time they are used in the text.

CHAPTER 1

Go, Danica!

The race cars zoomed around the track. It was a Sunday afternoon in Motegi, Japan. Eighteen drivers were competing in a race called the Indy Japan 300. Danica Patrick, the driver in the number 7 car, had never won an IndyCar race. IndyCar is a kind of professional racing between open-top cars with large wheels.

Danica was the only woman competing in the race that day. Being a woman in a sport made up mostly of men made her popular with fans. But it wasn't the only reason Danica was so well-known. She was a talented driver and a tough competitor. Danica was confident in her ability.

Danica speeds around the track in Motegi, Japan.

Chasing the Dream

For three years, Danica had tried to win her first IndyCar race. Many people thought a woman could never win. But Danica never stopped believing in herself. She knew her hard work would pay off one day.

Would April 20, 2008, finally be that day? Danica got off to a fast start in the race. She stayed close to the leaders. The first driver to complete 200 **laps**, or trips around the oval track, would win the race. During the 148th lap, Danica made her last **pit stop** to fill her car with fuel.

Racing to Win

With just 11 laps to go, Danica was in eighth place. She was running out of time. She quickly drove past a few cars to make her way to the front of the pack. During the 197th lap, Danica jumped from fourth to second place. She passed two drivers who had to make pit stops.

With just three laps to go, Danica sped into first place. She crossed the finish line more than 10 seconds ahead of the next driver. Danica had won the race!

Danica cried tears of joy. She thanked her family. She also thanked her racing team. They helped her **conserve**, or save, enough fuel to win the race. They also worked hard to make sure Danica's car was in the best shape for the race.

66When times are hard, you go a little harder. You don't give up. A lot of times, that is the difference.99

—Danica Patrick, after winning the Indy Japan 300

Danica celebrates after winning the Indy Japan 300. Helio Castroneves (left) finished in second place. Scott Dixon (right) came in third.

Victory Lap

Rival racer Helio Castroneves came in second place. He congratulated Danica on beating him and all the other men in the race. "She did a great job, passed me fair and square," he said.

It was a great day for Danica and a historic day in racing. Danica was the first woman ever to win an IndyCar race. It took years of hard work, dedication, and patience to do it. "We all have dreams at being the best at something," she said the day after the race. "Dreams really do come true."

Fast Fact

The name *Danica* means "morning star." As Danica's popularity soared, so did her name. After 2005, more new parents began to name their daughters Danica.

CHAPTER 2

Big Dreams

Danica's parents, T.J. and Bev, loved racing. T.J. raced snowmobiles and motocross bikes. He also raced small, powerful race cars called midget cars. Bev worked as a **mechanic**. They met at a snowmobile race and fell in love. Soon, they married and started a family.

Danica was born on March 25, 1982. She grew up in Roscoe, a small town in Illinois. Danica loved playing with dolls when she was a little girl. Thanks to her dad, she also loved learning about cars and the way they worked. Danica dreamed of winning the Indianapolis 500, the most famous race in America.

Two-year-old Danica (right) and her little sister, Brooke, smile for the camera. The sisters have always been very close.

A Rocky Start

When Danica was 10, she rode a **go-kart** for the first time. A friend of Danica's younger sister, Brooke, had one. At the time, Danica's parents were thinking of buying a boat. Brooke convinced them to buy go-karts instead.

The first time the sisters went go-kart racing, Danica crashed into a wall! Luckily, she was wearing a seat belt and helmet, so she didn't get hurt. After a few accidents, Brooke lost interest in racing. But Danica was hooked. "I was having fun and loved what I was doing," she said. The more she raced, the faster she got.

Danica gets ready to race at the 1993 World Karting Association Nationals in Jacksonville, Florida.

Finding a Groove

It wasn't long before Danica won her first go-kart race at a nearby track. She was in third place when two drivers crashed into each other. Danica steered around the crash and was the first to cross the finish line. "It felt awesome," Danica wrote. "I loved winning and I loved racing."

Breaking Ground

After a year of racing against boys at nearby tracks, Danica began traveling with her family to compete in other parts of the country. By age 11, Danica was breaking records on the track. By age 12, she won her first championship. In 1996, Danica won 39 of her 49 karting races! She won championship titles for four straight years, from 1994 through 1997.

Meeting a Mentor

Local newspapers started to write about Danica. She was invited to meet Lyn St. James, a famous female race-car driver. In 1992, St. James had made history by becoming the second woman to race in the Indianapolis 500.

St. James believed women could compete, and win, on the track. She created a program to help women learn to be great race-car drivers. Danica became one of her students. St. James was proud of Danica's performance on the track. She knew Danica was ready to take her racing to the next level.

Fast Fact

Famous race car drivers such as Michael Schumacher, Lewis Hamilton, and Jeff Gordon got their start in go-karts.

CHAPTER 3

Off to England

When Danica was 16, she was invited to race in England. Some of the world's best race-car drivers had gotten their start there. Danica was asked to participate in a racing **series** called Formula Vauxhall. This would be her first chance to switch from driving go-karts to real race cars.

Moving to England would mean leaving her family and friends. Danica was a junior at Hononegah High School. She was a cheerleader, and she played basketball and volleyball.

Danica poses in her high school cheerleading uniform. She liked cheerleading but not as much as racing.

A Big Decision

Danica knew she couldn't pass up the chance. "If I were truly pursuing my dream to someday win the Indy 500," she said, "England was my fastest path to get there."

After her third year of high school, Danica quit to follow her racing dream in England. At the airport, Danica's family cried. Danica was sad to be leaving her family, but she didn't cry. She couldn't wait to race in England!

Danica shows off her race car at the 1998 Formula Vauxhall Series in England.

Tough Times

Soon after Danica arrived in Milton Keynes, England, she was homesick. As the only girl in the racing series, Danica felt like an outsider. Sometimes she got into trouble. At first, that made her lose focus on racing. "Teenage boys can be pretty mean to a girl who is messing around in 'their' sport," Danica said.

On the track, Danica was slower than she had ever been. The **engineers** and mechanics who worked on race cars didn't pay much attention to her car. They didn't think Danica could win against the boys.

Back on Track

Back in Danica's hometown, her parents owned a glass company and a coffee shop. They worked hard to help pay for her to live and race in England. Danica was determined to get back on track and make them proud.

During Danica's first year in England, she finished ninth in the series. But she continued to improve. By her third season, in 2001, she was named the top up-and-coming road-racing driver. After three years away from home, Danica missed her family and friends. She decided it was time to come home.

Two Kinds of Racing

There are two styles of racing: open wheel and closed wheel. Open-wheel cars have big tires that are completely uncovered. IndyCar is the most popular type of open-wheel racing in the United States.

In closed-wheel racing, the cars look more like the ones you see on the road. NASCAR (right) is a type of closed-wheel racing.

CHAPTER 4

Entering the Big Leagues

While Danica lived in England, her driving got the attention of Bobby Rahal. He was a former champion driver. Rahal and television star David Letterman owned their own racing team in the United States. Rahal wanted to give Danica a chance to move up the racing ladder.

In 2003, Rahal formed a racing team just for Danica. She had a better car and more people on her team dedicated to help her win. This support helped Danica compete on a much tougher level.

Bobby Rahal stands with Danica and a crowd of reporters before a big race.

Joining the Team

Danica began racing in what was called the Toyota Atlantic Series. Before long, she was making headlines. At a race in Mexico, she finished in third place. That made her the first woman to stand on the **podium**, the place where a race's top three finishers are honored. At a race in Miami, Florida, Danica reached the podium again when she finished in second place.

Danica celebrates another proud moment. She finished in second place at the Toyota Atlantic race in Portland, Oregon in 2004.

Ready for the IRL

During her second season, Danica continued to do well. By the end of the 2004 season, Rahal announced Danica was ready to drive in the Indy Racing League (IRL). That was big news! Danica would be racing against some of the world's best drivers. She was about to become the first woman to drive full-time in the IRL.

During her first IRL race, Danica crashed her car. But that didn't stop her. By her fourth race, Danica finished in fourth place. Fans were excited to see a woman do so well in her **rookie** year.

Fast Fact

In 2004, Danica was the only driver in the Toyota Atlantic Series to complete every lap of every race in the season.

A Dream Come True

On May 29, 2005, Danica prepared to race in the famous Indianapolis 500. This was the race she dreamed about as a kid. Danica was just 23 years old, but she had already made history. She was only the fourth woman ever to compete in the race. Until the 1970s, women weren't even allowed on the track, unless they were watching a race.

All About Indy

The Indianapolis 500 is the most famous car race in the United States. Drivers must complete 200 laps around an oval-shaped track. Each lap covers a distance of 2.5 miles (4 kilometers). All together, drivers must race for 500 miles (805 km).

The first Indy 500 was held in 1911. Over the years, it has become more and more popular. The race draws more than 350,000 people to the Indianapolis Motor Speedway. That's the largest attendance of any sporting event held in a single day.

Women at the Indy 500

In 1997, Janet Guthrie became the first women to drive in the Indy 500. She was followed by Lyn St. James in 1992 and Sarah Fisher in 2000. Danica was the fourth female driver to race at Indy.

Milka Duno, Sarah Fisher, and Lyn St. James

In 2007, Milka Duno became the fifth woman to start the famous race. That year, Danica, Fisher, and Duno all competed in the race. It was the first time in history that three of the race's 33 drivers were women! Today, all three women continue to make news for their racing.

Historic Start

"Lady and gentlemen, start your engines!" said the Indianapolis Motor Speedway chairperson at the start of the race. The "lady" in the race was Danica. During the 57th lap, Danica moved into first place. For the first time ever, a woman was leading the Indy 500! Her fans cheered, "D-A-N-I-C-A!"

Pit Stop Panic

For 19 laps, Danica remained in the lead. During the 79th lap, she made a pit stop for fuel and dropped to 16th place. But she quickly made up some of the ground she had lost. Her fans kept cheering. Danica took the lead again with just 10 laps to go. But her car was low on fuel, and there was no time left to make another pit stop.

Danica leads the pack at the 2005 Indianapolis 500. No woman has ever done better in the famous race.

Strong Finish

Danica got the news over the radio from her chief engineer, Ray Leto. She had to slow down to save fuel. Three drivers passed Danica, and she ended up in fourth place. Even though she didn't win, Danica was proud. Her finish was the best ever by a woman.

Danica couldn't help but think back to when she was a little girl with a big dream. "I always knew I'd someday drive in the Indy 500," Danica said.

What Does the Pit Crew Do?

When Danica makes a pit stop, members of her pit crew quickly get to work. They fill her car with fuel and change its tires. They also make any needed changes to the engine to improve the car's performance.

The pit crew gets a lot done in very little time. The average pit stop lasts from 10 and 14 seconds! Danica says, "The outcome of each race is dependent on every member of my team working in sync."

> **❝**I knew from my earliest childhood memories that I would make a name for myself as a professional race-car driver.**❞**
>
> —Danica Patrick

A New Star

Danica's strong race performance made her an instant celebrity. Her good looks—on top of her talent—made her even more popular. Newspapers and TV shows lined up to interview her.

On July 2, 2005, Danica won her first **pole position**. She drove the fastest in a series of timed practice runs before the race. That allowed her to start the race from the first position, an advantage for a driver. She was just the second woman to "win the pole." The first was Sarah Fisher in 2002 at Kentucky Speedway.

By the end of the season, Danica was named the 2005 IndyCar Rookie of the Year. She proved she was much more than a pretty face in the world of racing.

Fast Fact

Danica was the first IndyCar driver, man or woman, to appear on the cover of *Sports Illustrated*.

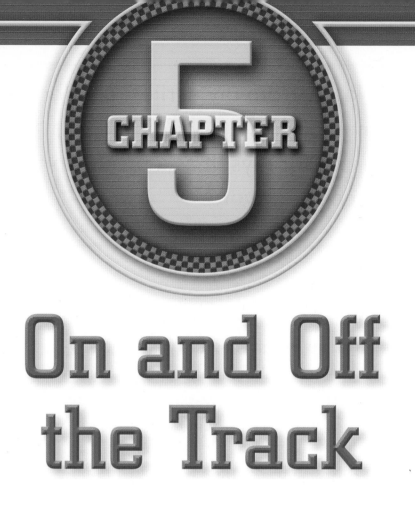

CHAPTER 5

On and Off the Track

Growing up, Danica dreamed of the day she would marry "Mr. Right." She met Paul Hospenthal in 2001, after she hurt herself while doing a type of exercise called **yoga**. He was a **physical therapist** who worked with athletes. Paul and Danica fell in love.

On Thanksgiving Day in 2004, Paul asked Danica to marry him. "Yes! Yes! Yes!" Danica screamed in delight. One year later, in November 2005, they were married.

Happy Family

Danica and Paul live in Scottsdale, Arizona, with their dog, a miniature schnauzer named William Robert. His nickname is Billy. Danica loves spending time at home with Paul and Billy. "Home is a peaceful place in my otherwise hectic life," Danica says.

Paul and Danica pose together at the 2006 ESPY Awards.

Because of her racing schedule, Danica spends more than half of every year away from home. Her parents and Paul travel to all of her races. They help Danica feel at home when she's on the road. They also help her stay focused on her goal: winning races. At the end of the 2006 season, Danica decided to move to a new team. She hoped this would increase her chances of winning.

Danica chats with her Andretti Green teammates in 2006 (from left): Tony Kanaan, Bryan Herta, and Dario Franchitti.

New Partners

Danica joined the Andretti Green Racing team, partly owned by the world-famous Andretti family. As part of her new team, Danica would drive the most powerful race car of her life.

Racing for Andretti Green, Danica finished the 2007 season in seventh place. It was the best finish in her career to that point. Still, many people questioned whether a female driver would ever win a race. On April 20, 2008, Danica had an answer—yes! She won her first race with the Andretti Green team at the Indy Japan 300.

What Are Racing Sponsors?

Why do drivers have all those patches and brand names on their racing suits and cars? Operating a racing team costs a lot of money. One of the main ways teams raise money is with the help of **sponsors**.

Sponsors give a driver's team money. In return, the driver agrees to wear the company's name on his or her driving suit. Drivers also appear at major events held by sponsors. Those events give drivers a chance to show support for a sponsor. The events also help raise awareness of a company or product. In exchange, racing teams earn enough money to pay for better cars and equipment.

Moving Forward

Each race is a new challenge. "I still have the same nerves before every race that I had before I won," Danica says. "I want to win races."

Some races are tougher than others. On May 25, 2008, Danica failed to finish the Indy 500 for the first time. She was in the top 10 for most of the race, but she was forced out after another driver hit her car. Danica was disappointed. But she didn't let that "bump in the road" stop her from trying harder the next time.

Fast Fact

Danica keeps fit and prepares for her races by running, lifting weights, and doing yoga.

Danica signs autographs for young fans. She hopes to inspire more girls to get into racing.

Role Model

With her first win behind her, Danica has a new goal. She hopes to win an IndyCar championship. The driver with the best performance during a season wins the championship title. Danica also still dreams of winning the Indy 500.

As a girl, Danica was inspired by women race-car drivers. Now she hopes to be a role model for girls. Danica says, "It's a role I am prepared for if it means more young women grow up believing they can do anything, be anyone, and achieve everything they aim for."

Time Line

1982 — Danica is born on March 25 in Beloit, Wisconsin.

1992 — At age 10, Danica begins racing go-karts.

1997 — Danica wins the World Karting Association Grand National Championship.

1998 — Danica begins racing in England.

2002 — Danica joins a team put together by former race-car driver Bobby Rahal.

2004 — Danica becomes the first woman to win a pole position in a Toyota Atlantic Series race.

2005 — Danica finishes fourth in the Indianapolis 500. She marries physical therapist Paul Hospenthal.

2008 — Danica becomes the first woman to win an IndyCar race with her victory in Motegi, Japan.

Glossary

conserve: to avoid waste by using carefully

engineer: a person who designs, builds, and tests race cars

go-kart: a small, one-person racing vehicle with a motor

lap: one complete time around a racetrack

mechanic: a person who repairs cars

physical therapist: a person who treats pain and disease by using massage, exercise, heat, and other methods

pit stop: a stop during a race to fill a car with fuel, change its tires, or make repairs

podium: a special platform where the top three finishers in a race stand to receive their awards

pole position: the first starting position in a race, given to the driver who performs best in a series of qualifying rounds

rookie: describes an athlete in his or her first season as a professional

series: a group of races

sponsor: a person or business that pays a race-car driver's team in exchange for advertising on the driver's car and driving suit

yoga: a system of exercise that involves holding poses and stretching while doing controlled breathing

Find Out More

Books

Braulick, Carrie A. *Indy Cars*. Minneapolis: Capstone Press, 2006.

Mello, Tara Baukus. *Danica Patrick*. Race Car Legends. New York: Chelsea House, 2007.

Piehl, Janet. *Indy Race Cars*. Motor Mania. Minneapolis: Lerner, 2007.

Web Sites

Danica Patrick
www.danicaracing.com

The Indianapolis 500
www.indy500.com

The IndyCar Racing Series
www.indycar.com

Source Notes

pp. 6, 7 (bottom): Martin, Bruce. "Patrick Finally Answers Her Critics." sportsillustrated.cnn.com. April 21, 2008. sportsillustrated.cnn.com/2008/writers/bruce_martin/04/21/patrick

p. 7 (top): Associated Press.

pp. 9, 10, 13, 14, 20, 22, 23, 24, 25, 28: Patrick, Danica with Laura Morton. *Danica Crossing the Line*. New York: Fireside, 2006.

p. 27: Story, Mark. "Danica returning to state a winner." kentucky.com. August 1, 2008. www.kentucky.com/287/story/477050.html

Index

About the Author

Dina El Nabli is a writer, an online editor, and the author of children's biographies of Eleanor Roosevelt and Henry Ford. She lives in New Jersey with her husband, Khaled, a loyal Formula 1 fan and want-to-be race-car driver, and her son, Ryan, whose favorite toys all have wheels.